ON BORDER
The Way of The Cross

NEW MEXICO — EL PASO
MEXICO

Sister Evangeline Salazar, OSB

Copyright ©2020 Sister Evangeline Salazar, OSB
All Rights Reserved

LEGAL DISCLAIMER: No part of this book may be reproduced or transmitted in any form or by any means, electronic or mechanical, including photocopying, recording or by any information storage and retrieval system, without written permission from the author. You may not reprint, resell or distribute the contents of this book without express written permission from the author.

All violations will be remedied with legal action and justice will be sought to the maximum penalty allowable by law in the State in which the original purchaser resides.

Design: Liz Mrofka, What If? Publishing
Printed by: Kindle Direct Publishing

Benet Hill Monastery
of Colorado Springs, Inc.
3190 Benet Lane
Colorado Springs, Colorado 80921

ISBN-13: 979-8628290002

PRAISE

"Sister Evangeline's stories of light and faith in the lives of these immigrants who are seeking a better life for their children and themselves have moved me to tears."

—Sister Clare Carr, Prioress

"Hi Evangeline,

I must say that your writing is beautiful. I don't know if you write every day or just occasionally, but I would be interested in everything you have to share regarding your experiences. I am so impressed at your tender heart and love for the work you do. Thank you for sharing this with me. You have a true gift of making a connection with the heart in your writing and how you relate it to your personal reflections-simply beautiful!

I am going to share it with our constituents, but I was thinking in parts- like an on-going story that keeps the issue alive and vibrant in the mind of the reader."

Let me know-Blessings,
—Gina Berger, Communications Director,
Benet Hill Monastery

REF: Radio Interview on Colorado Public Radio

"Sister Evangeline's reflection on Veronica is truly inspired. I have never thought of having a favorite Station of the Cross. Now I have one. I wasn't aware of how many shoes I have. Now I am. Evangeline's humility, generosity and compassion will reach many. May our nation find a way to show such hospitality to those who have so much faith and hope in an American way of life."

—Hugh Burns, Friend of Benet Hill

DEDICATION

To the children on the border, in cages and separated from their families in the hope that someday soon they will be reunited.

To my brother, Severo (1938-2019), who paid me to do his writing assignments in high school in the belief that I needed the practice and he didn't.

I also dedicate this book to my mentor and friend, Sister Jeremy Dempsey, who taught me the value and depth of the written word.

TOP LEFT: Game time with the children.
TOP RIGHT: Juana writing her story.
BELOW: Breaking bread with refugees and immigrants.

TABLE OF CONTENTS

Acknowledgments..6

Forward..7

Introduction...8

About the Author..10

The First Station: Jesus is Condemned to Die..................12

The Second Station: Jesus Carries His Cross..................16

The Third Station: Jesus Falls the First Time................20

The Fourth Station: Jesus Meets His Blessed Mother...........24

The Fifth Station: Simon of Cyrene Helps Jesus Carry the Cross..28

The Sixth Station: Veronica Washes the Face of Jesus.........32

The Seventh Station: Jesus Falls the Second Time.............36

The Eighth Station: Jesus Speaks to the Women................40

The Ninth Station: Jesus Falls the Third Time................44

The Tenth Station: Jesus is Stripped of His Garments.........48

The Eleventh Station: Jesus is Nailed to the Cross...........52

The Twelfth Station: Jesus Dies on the Cross.................56

The Thirteenth Station: Jesus is Taken Down from the Cross...60

The Fourteenth Station: Jesus is Laid in the Tomb............64

The Fifteenth Station: The Resurrection of Jesus - Part 1....68

The Fifteenth Station: The Resurrection of Jesus - Part 2....72

ACKNOWLEDGMENTS

With the encouragement of Sister Clare, our prioress, and the sisters of our community, I was able respond to the call to serve the immigrants, refugees, and asylum seekers on our Southern border. I especially want to thank Sister Buffy Boesen, SL for the hospitality she provided at the Loretto convent. Special thanks to Blanca Arellano, Susie, Leroy, and Emilio Trujillo who provided me with help and space when the work became especially heavy. Special blessings to the many sisters from many communities who responded to the call and helped build community in El Paso.

Thanks to these Benedictine sisters, both living and deceased, who helped with the carving of The Stations of the Cross; Sisters Anselm Chastain, Katie Keeley, Julia Wilkinson, Marita Law, Sophie Glenski, Anastasia Wabs, Irmina Miller, Amanda Hermesch, Guadalupe Manchego, and Devota Klamet.

Don Becker and Jim Buxton who helped in the restoration process. Carlos and Dodi Ortega who created the cases for protecting the Stations. Patrick Bussell and Thomas Sheehan who helped by hanging the Stations on the trees.

I am especially grateful to Sonja Ragaller, Sister Naomi Rosenberger, OSB and Barbara Neilon for their great job of editing. Thanks to Gina Berger for her encouragement to keep the book alive.

To Haley Sanchez, I owe a debt of gratitude for the interview on CPR. Thanks also to Sister Lynn McKenzie, OSB, President of the Federation of St. Scholastica, for providing the LCWR and the Federation of St. Scholastica with the link to the interview.

FORWARD

Sister Evangeline Salazar, OSB (Vangie) is an old friend and we share a lot of history together. Most memorable from early years is our joint work in peace and social justice witnessing to the Catholic bishops followed by a weeklong witness at the Pentagon during the Vietnam War. I have seen Vangie sporadically through the years, because she lived in Albuquerque working with the Hispanic residents while I was in Washington, D.C. teaching religious studies at the Catholic University and giving talks around the country on social justice.

When we reconnected, the U.S. Government was restricting Mexican immigrants and building the border wall. Vangie came out of retirement and returned to the borders at the time Mexican and Central American families were being separated and asylum seekers were being isolated in detention camps. As a native Spanish speaker, born in a Hispanic community in southwest Colorado, Vangie was able to communicate colloquially with migrants from Mexico and Central America.

News media have not yet picked up on the collaboration of hundreds of Catholic sisters at the border providing shelter, food, clothing, and local transportation to immigrants and asylum seekers, often at their own expense. Their story has not yet been widely told. My friend and compatriot, a young 80-year old sister, tells her story about how her life and prayer have been impacted by recent encounters with her American and Hispanic sisters and brothers. May her telling of this tale change and move hearts, that have so far remained indifferent.

Mary Collins, OSB
Emerita Professor of Religious Studies
The Catholic University of America
Past Coordinator of Benedictines for Peace

INTRODUCTION

In carving the STATIONS OF THE CROSS and in writing REFLECTIONS FROM EL PASO, I spent precious moments in the presence of our Lord and Savior Jesus Christ. In putting these two experiences together, I have attempted to give the reader a sense of what a transformative experience walking the Way of the Cross and ministering to refugees, immigrants, and asylum seekers can be.

In 1968, Benet Hill Monastery was a very young community and I was a very young sister. On one of her visits to our small community in Walsenburg, Colorado, Mother Liguori asked Sister Anselm Chastain to carve the Stations of the Cross for our new cemetery in the Black Forest. Sister Anselm accepted the assignment and solicited the help of Sister Sharon Murray, Sister Julia Wilkinson, and me.

Mother Liguori presented us with some soft red wood left over from the construction of the pews in the chapel. Sister Sharon created 18 by 24-inch sketches of each of the 14 Stations of the Cross. Sister Anselm carved the first station: Jesus is condemned to die and station four: Jesus meets His sorrowful mother. I carved station two: Jesus takes up His cross and station three: Jesus falls the first time.

Sister Anselm left the community and went back to Atchison. I was left with ten unfinished pieces of wood. I carried them with me everywhere I went, soliciting help from every sister I encountered. No one wanted to take on the burden of carving an entire station, so I carved the main parts and other sisters helped by scraping off the excess wood. In time, Sister Anastasia completed the ninth station: Jesus falls the third time. Sister Katie Keeley completed stations ten, eleven, and twelve. I completed thirteen and fourteen in 1975. All the stations were hung on trees leading to the cemetery the following year.

When I returned to the forest after twenty years of ministry in Albuquerque, I found what weather, bugs, and birds can do to a fine piece of wood. I was devastated. I took the stations down and started two years of restoration. This was not an easy job as much of the original carvings were almost destroyed. With the help of some of the sisters, friends, and neighbors I restored the stations to their pristine beauty.

I carved the fifteenth station in 2016. Carlos and Dodi Ortega, friends from Albuquerque, designed and constructed glassed-in frames to preserve the work.

On November 15, 2019, I traveled to El Paso, Texas in answer to a call from the Leadership Conference of Women Religious and the invitation from my Prioress, Sister Clare Carr, to help with the refugee crisis on our Southern Border.

If carving and restoring the Stations of the Cross was a transforming experience, you can only imagine the transformation that took place in my heart and soul as I walked daily with the poorest of the poor. These men, women, and children opened my heart to the fullness of the suffering of Christ. My prayer for you is in seeing these pictures and reading and meditating on these humble reflections you, too, may be transformed and moved to do whatever is in your power to bring about the kingdom of God here on Earth. God bless you.

TOP LEFT: Julio presents Sister Evangeline with a rosary, handmade by his abuela.
TOP RIGHT: Drawings by the children.

ABOUT THE AUTHOR

EVANGELINE SALAZAR is a Benedictine Sister and a member of the Benet Hill Monastery community. Responding to the call of the poor, the hungry, and oppressed, she ministered to the people in Nicaragua, El Salvador, Guatemala, Columbia, and Guantanamo Bay. Presently, at the age of eighty, she is a volunteer with Annunciation House in El Paso, Texas, ministering to asylum seekers released from the detention centers. She was instrumental with the community in sponsoring asylum seekers, Frank and Louisa Dominguez Rojas from Cuba.

Evangeline earned a bachelor's degree at Mt. St. Scholastica College and a master's degree in education at the University of Colorado. She learned to carve after she found a small knife and a piece of wood and put them together to create a beautiful puppy.

FIRST STATION
JESUS IS CONDEMNED TO DIE

1 'm freezing sitting out here in the hall. I'm staying in a drafty, old convent pretty much like the old convent in Atchison where I lived as a young sister. As a matter of fact, it feels like the old 3rd floor, brown wood trim, gray walls, and rickety old stairs. I asked them to turn up the heat. They have it up to 70 degrees, but it doesn't help much because all the warm air goes to the high ceilings.

I experienced a great joy when I ran into Patricia from Atchison on my way to the communal bathroom. It took me a moment to recognize her. It didn't even take her a moment to recognize me. I also met their postulant, Molly. To add to the joy, we were assigned to work on the same team. They rented a car for $400.00 dollars a week which they thought was a bargain. I benefited because I got to ride to and from the place where we were processing the refugees. I did translations and paperwork, met with each family member, and asked the necessary questions to get them connected to their sponsors.

The sponsors needed to know the refugees were here so they could send plane or bus tickets. I had to connect with the sponsors who spoke Spanish and very little English.

Yesterday, my first day on the job, was tiring beyond my imagination. We worked straight from two in the afternoon to ten at night. We didn't even have time to eat or go to the bathroom. The people arrived; we were on high alert. The refugees arrived, cold, hungry, and needing to go to the bathroom. They had to form a line (stand in the cold parking lot) so we could care for each family, one at a time.

We had three persons doing the paperwork and manning the phones. We worked in limited space with only three phones and one bathroom; the workspace was crazy! We got all the answers to the usual questions: Name? Where did you come from? Birth date? Age? Who is with you? Finally, where are you going and who is your sponsor? We recorded the same information for each child. Next we called the sponsors on behalf of the individuals they were sponsoring. We gave the sponsor the information needed to purchase a plane or bus ticket. We then let them talk to each other. We asked the sponsor to let us know when travel arrangements were made, hopefully by the next day. It was a slow process indeed.

As we finished, another member of the team matched them with a room. Most families had to share a room. Motel rooms have only one or two beds. We tried not to mix the sexes. Father and a son had to be matched with a father and a son. The problem came towards the end when what we had left was a mother with a son or a father with a daughter. We did what we could. We only had one family with a father, mother, and a child.

Next was serving a meal. We had a large tent on the parking lot. Tables, chairs, and portable heaters were set up in the tent. Volunteers prepared the food and drinks, served and cleaned up. That part went well.

After the people were fed, they were given a change of clothing, and a packet of necessary items (soap, toothpaste, tooth brush, etc.) Finally, the people went to their rooms where they could bathe, sleep, and dream of a land of milk and honey.

Our work was not finished for the day. We started receiving calls from the sponsors detailing travel plans and marked them to deliver in the morning.

Finally, at 10 PM, we headed for a night of rest. I fell into bed, tired, and worn out wondering what I had signed up for. I will say, I fell in love with the Jesus in each person, tired, hungry, cold, and with a smile that stole my heart. The poor in their joyful hope were truly a blessing to me.

Estoy fuera de otro día de amor. *I'm off to another day of love.*

—Bendiciones para todos. *Blessings to all.*

REFLECTION QUESTION

Jesus is Condemned:
How do I participate in the power structures that allow people to be unjustly condemned?

REFLECTIONS

SECOND STATION
JESUS CARRIES HIS CROSS

Talk about hectic! Oh, my sweet, sweet Jesus. I was put in charge of the receiving room today. We were given phones and two desks in a tiny room with a bed that takes up half the space. Eighty families arrived at 2:30 PM just as my shift began.

Let me tell you how this works. ICE releases these people after they have been in detention for only God knows how long. They are released onto the street with only the clothes on their backs. ICE informs us that they are releasing several persons. That helps us determine how many buses to send to pick them up. We receive them one family or person at a time. We ask them the questions necessary to help us contact the person who is sponsoring them. This takes a certain amount of time; to ask the questions, write the answers down, and call their sponsor. Six people talk at the same time in a tiny crowed space. Once we have contacted the sponsor, we ask them to purchase a plane or bus ticket and call us back with the confirmation number. Next, they wait for us to call and inform them when they are leaving. We then feed them and give them a change of clothes. They are now free to bathe or shower. Next, they wait for us to call them to tell them we have heard from their sponsors, and we tell them when they are leaving. When their time comes, we give them a backpack with food and the items they need for travel.

During the waiting period they are free to do whatever they wish. We have toys and coloring books for the children. The adults mostly watch the children. While they wait, we feed them three times a day and provide whatever they need: soap, shampoo, toothbrush and toothpaste, etc.

Last night we received a call from the sponsor of a woman traveling with her child by plane. The uncle was waiting at the airport and she did not arrive. Luckily for all of us, she was able to get a phone to call her uncle. Meanwhile, the uncle called to tell us the plane had a problem. Everyone was asked to deplane and were told they could purchase a bus or train ticket to take them to their destination. The woman had no money, didn't know where she was, and had only a limited time to use the phone. So, what can we do? Absolutely nothing. What a heart-breaking story! We pray she can find a kind person who understands Spanish and is willing to help refugees.

The one good thing for her is she knows her uncle's phone number. Most of the religious communities have sent two sisters to help. Most don't speak Spanish. We really need someone with organizational skills such as Sister Naomi. Many sisters are helping in the clothing section and others are helping in the assignment of rooms. Anyone who speaks Spanish is doing what I am doing.

All adults have ankle monitors because they will have a court hearing to determine if they get to stay in this country or be deported. To top this craziness, the place where they are staying is not the same place for their hearing. Anything to make it harder for these poor people.

I was not as tired last night, my back did not hurt, but my right knee/leg was ready to give out. I'm taking my cane today just in case I need it. I think you should consider coming to help me, Sister Naomi.

The people of El Paso need to be recognized for all they are doing to help the refugees. These amazing volunteers cook, clean, run shuttles, collect, and donate all the items we give the people, etc.

¡Dios los bendiga a todos, mucho amor y paz!
God bless us everyone, much love and peace!

REFLECTION QUESTION

Jesus Carries His Cross:
I have been given a cross not of my choosing.
How do I carry it?

REFLECTIONS

THIRD STATION
JESUS FALLS THE FIRST TIME

Good morning all. Another blessed and hectic day in the El Paso receiving station. We arrived at 2 PM to find out the guests had not been fed properly and the volunteers in charge failed to provide the food. Miracles of miracles, my friend Blanca Arellano and her daughter Susie, arrived with all the makings for quesadillas and horchata. What a treat! Like Jesus feeding the 5000, we were able to feed the 90. What a blessing my friends have been!

Once the people are connected with their sponsors, tickets purchased, and we know the destination and time of departure, we provide transportation to the bus station or the airport. Because the shuttles only operate at certain times, it may be necessary for some people to spend the night in the airport or the bus station.

A lovely woman named Victoria and her child were very frightened of traveling by bus. She was afraid she would miss her bus because she had to transfer from one bus to another to reach her final destination. We tried to assure her there would be people to help her along the way, and signs would be posted in English and Spanish. She couldn't read but the daughter could, so we worked out a plan for them. We fell in love with this woman and child. Blanca and Susie decided they didn't want them to spend the night in the bus station. Instead they would pick her up in the morning and take her to the bus station. I was in charge, so I told them it was an OK thing to do. All arrangements were made. At 8:30 PM, Mary, the top boss, came to take the family. I explained what we had planned, but she negated the whole plan. In the end, she took the family to the bus station. I had to call my friends and explain the situation. It broke my heart, but rules are rules. There is always someone with more authority. Such is life.

Estamos en camino a la Misa. *We are on our way to Mass.*
Los amo. *Love you.*

REFLECTION QUESTION

Jesus Falls the First Time:
When I fail, how do I rise again?

REFLECTIONS

REFLECTIONS

FOURTH STATION
JESUS MEETS HIS BLESSED MOTHER

The flight to El Paso was uneventful; everything happened as scheduled. I took the front seat, wore a mask, and coughed less. Sleep, however, eluded me. I tried praying the rosary and that helped.

My friends, Susie, Leroy, and their son Mando, met me and took me to a nice Italian restaurant for salad and pizza. I couldn't believe how delicious everything tasted after two weeks of not being able to taste anything.

On arriving in my room, I was pleasantly surprised to discover the warmth radiating from within. It was wonderful not to enter a cold room.

In the late morning, Susie picked me up for a wonderful breakfast at the Village Inn. The coffee was to die for! Next, we went to Albertsons for some needed grocery shopping. Sugar Flakes, milk, bread, butter, avocado, mango, tortillas, apples, bananas in honor of Annie the banana, cheese and turkey from the deli, orange juice, and a piece of chocolate for a treat. I'm not a great shopper but I managed to buy some of my favorite things.

Nazareth is a much more organized place to work. My type of work area: everything has a place and everything in its place. Nazareth is the Sisters of Loretto's former nursing home. We have plenty of room to house and care for 100 refugees at a time. We have a big dining room, a large recreation room, about 40 bedrooms, two storage rooms for clothing, one room for medical supplies, and a room for preparing the back packs. Best of all, each of us who interview the refugees have an office-like space where we can use the telephone and talk to people without interfering noise. Yes!

I worked from 2 to 10 PM. First I met the refugees and talked to them a bit and listened to their stories. I filled out the forms, called the sponsors, let the refugees talk to their sponsors, posted the information, filled in for the nurse, and distributed medicine to sick babies, hurting children, and aching adults.

It was a bone-weary day and with the grace of my Lord and Savior Jesus Christ, I was able to feed the hungry, calm the fears of the weary, clothe the naked, heal the sick, and bring some joy and laughter to my helpers in the vineyard of the Lord.

Dios nos bendiga a todos. *God bless us everyone.*

REFLECTION QUESTION

Jesus Meets His Blessed Mother:
Jesus looks into His mother's eyes and pleads,
"I'm sorry for the pain I am causing you, please let me do this, let me go."
How do I let go of a love so deep?

REFLECTIONS

FIFTH STATION
SIMON OF CYRENE HELPS JESUS CARRY THE CROSS

I have often wondered what passed between their eyes when Jesus met His Mother on the way to Calvary. Did He think, "I'm so sorry, Mother dear. I have caused you so much pain because I have loved so many and so much." And His brokenhearted Mother, what passed through her heart? "My darling Son, did I fail you in any way?" My thoughts swirl around mother and son as I minister to these young mothers and their children. Many are helpless but never hopeless.

Bone-weary tired, I fall into bed thinking of all the Simons in my life. Jesus is bone-weary tired as He carries His cross through the streets of Jerusalem. Suddenly Simon appears to help carry the burden. Today we were at the point of exhaustion when Brother Juan appeared at our doorstep and offered to lift some of the burden from our shoulders. The weariness comes from the fact that so many of the refugees arrive with very sick children and babies. We don't know how to help. We don't know what to give them to relieve their sickness or their pain. We have a lot of over-the-counter medicine, but what to give for what is the question. Brother Juan is a nurse and works at a nearby hospital. Today, he was inspired to come and see how he could help. Within moments, he separated and labeled the different types of medicine. Gracias a Dios for small miracles.

So, my dear friends, the work of the Lord continues. I thought this morning as I lay in bed, struggling to get up, what is it about these people that compels my heart to respond with love and respect? What is it about these people that moves me to tears as I witness their suffering? What is the gift they bring to me? In truth, I believe, these were the ones to whom Jesus ministered to in His day. I see these people following Jesus as He preached the Good News. Poor people, hungry, dirty, smelly, sick people following a dream. People who need to be fed because they were not smart enough to pack a lunch as they set out to follow a Vision.

A gentleman in one of the offices here at Loretto offered me a cup of coffee. The ministry of the Lord is universal. Unknowingly, we often minister to one another.

Dios los bendiga, mis amados amigos y familiares. Yo deseo que Jesús les de un dia Lleno de Paz y Alegría. *God bless you, my lovely friends and family. I wish for you a Jesus Day Full of Peace and Joy.*

REFLECTION QUESTION

Simon of Cyrene Helps Jesus Carry the Cross:
How do I respond to the blind, the cripple, the refugee; the person whose cross seems to be more than I can carry?

REFLECTIONS

SIXTH STATION
VERONICA WASHES THE FACE OF JESUS

One thing you may or may not know about me, since I have aged a little, my tear ducts don't close completely and tears often drip off the side of my face. If I don't bother to wipe them off immediately, they tend to crust on the side of my face. Yesterday, as I sat with the father of a three-year-old child, I felt a small hand rubbing the side of my face. I looked up, smiled at the boy, and smiling back at me he said, "crusty" in Spanish.

I could not take my eyes off of him. I was so taken up by this small gesture of love. Imagine, a three-year-old noticing a crust on the side of your face and reaching out his small hand to wipe it away. I was moved to new tears. As I held the child in my arms, my thoughts turned to Veronica wiping the face of Jesus on the way to Calvary. What did that small gesture mean to the Son of God? Walking slowly on a dirty, dusty road, His face sweaty, dirty and itching, and along comes a young woman, risking her life to wipe the face of Jesus!

Today was one of those days. The people arrived, dirty, smelly, hungry, and needing to go to the bathroom. We waited for them with what little we had: a clean washcloth to wipe their faces and hands. It is amazing how a clean, cool washcloth can lift the spirits of the tired and weary. We had a nice, healthy lunch for them which they ate with great enthusiasm. In this environment, it doesn't take much to be grateful for whatever God, through the hands of kindness, provides.

Yo deseo alegría. *I wish you joy.*
Yo deseo su salud. *I wish you health.*
Yo deseo su paz, amabilidad y bondad. *I wish you peace and kindness and goodness.*

—*Evangeline*

REFLECTION QUESTION

Veronica Washes the Face of Jesus:
How do I respond to the people who carry
so much pain and so much sorrow?

REFLECTIONS

REFLECTIONS

SEVENTH STATION
JESUS FALLS THE SECOND TIME

It is with a heavy heart I leave work today. We had 400 people released today. Among the 10 receiving places we operate, we could only accommodate 335. What happened to the other 65? When ICE releases these people, they are simply put out on the street to fend for themselves. We pick them up according to how many each of us can reasonably accommodate. We have 50 beds or cots; two in each room. We house two adults and two children in each room. Each child sleeps with his/her parent no matter the age of the child. We try very hard not to mix the sexes. Sometimes this proves to be an insurmountable problem. We do the best we can.

Today was one of those days we simply couldn't do enough. "We had no room in the inn." Can you imagine how painful these words are to those of us who dedicate our lives to making room for everyone?

When I was carving the seventh station, I often wondered how Jesus felt as he kept falling on His way to Calvary. Tonight, I ask, my Lord and Savior Jesus Christ, "How did it feel, to fall and fall again?" "Did you ever stop to think you might not make it?" "Did it occur to you, sweet, sweet Jesus, as you lay prostrate on the ground, that you might not have the strength to complete the journey?" "That you might not be able to save us all?" "And what if you could only save a few of us?" "What about the 65, outside, cold and hungry, and needing to go to the bathroom?"

Tomorrow, thank God, is another day. The sun will rise and warm the streets. We will awake with renewed strength and a brighter vision. We will rise with you, Jesus, and know that you have cared for those we could not.

Amén *Amen*
Bendito sea Dios. *Blessed Be God.*

—*Evangeline*

REFLECTION QUESTION

Jesus Falls the Second Time:
Not again! I must get up. What is it that will motivate me to pick myself up and start again?

REFLECTIONS

REFLECTIONS

EIGHTH STATION
JESUS SPEAKS TO THE WOMEN

To whom does Jesus speak? Who are these women? Where are these women? Walking this lonely, rugged trail, Jesus must have thought about all the important people in His life. Why do these women stand out? Because they were there. These were the women who always stood by His side. They were the women who attended Him, served Him, listened to Him, and called Him to the service of others. I have met these women in many walks of my life.

More recently, I have met them in the halls of Loretto, in the kitchens of Nazareth, in the offices, in the hallways, in the dining rooms, under the tents, and in the bedrooms of the refugees who arrive on a daily basis. These are the women who responded to the call from the Leadership Conference of Women Religious (LCWR). Two by two the sisters arrived at Loretto and sometimes one or three: Patricia and Mollie, Benedictines from Atchison; Lucille and Clarita, Franciscans from New York; Betty and Sylvia, Sisters of Notre Dame from Kentucky; Rita, Judy, Marcia, Brenda, Maria, Lupe, and so many others from many different communities. Lovely women, kind and compassionate, always willing to lend a hand at whatever needs to be done in the moment.

We speak the language of the people; Spanish, English, sign, and sometimes we just act it out, whatever works. We are a happy, joyful group. We share our space, our food, our work, and our song. Our hearts bleed for the many women we serve; women who come to look for freedom, women with a dream in their hearts, women who come to escape violence and abuse, women who want a better future for their children. No woman comes alone; every woman carries a babe in arms or brings a toddler barely walking, a twelve-year-old, or a teenager. It's hard to imagine what these women have experienced. These, too, are the women Jesus meets on His way to the Cross.

There are other women on the road like Blanca Arellano. She kindly invited me to her home for a good night's rest, gave me a ride to El Paso, and offered a couple of days' help with our work. Susie, her daughter, and Susie's lovely husband, Leroy, and their son, Emilio, also invited me into their home for a good night's sleep and a few hours of "Madam Secretary". My very good friend, Ana Bruciaga, who invited me to Chihuahua for the week-end and cleaned up the mess when I got violently sick. What an angel of God! Dr. Alma cared for me with such special love, kindness, and compassion.

Jesus speaks to the women of the world, this small world we live in. We are demonstrating that women caring for women is our call and our response. I thank the women in my community for the life they give me in being one of them.

Te deseo paz y alegría, salud y el don de lagrimas en un corazon compasivo y amor sin limites.
I wish you peace and joy, health and the gift of tears, a compassionate heart, and love without bounds.

—*Evangeline*

REFLECTION QUESTION

Jesus Speaks to the Women:
You are woman; you are strong.
What motivates me to take a stand and be counted?

REFLECTIONS

NINTH STATION
JESUS FALLS THE THIRD TIME

Sister Anastasia carved the Ninth Station. If you look at all the stations, it is the one most different from all the rest. It is my favorite for many reasons besides the beautiful carving. In attempting to "fix" it after the woodpeckers had eaten so much of it, I had to take great pains to not change it from its original composition.

Jesus falls the third time! How many times do I fail in the promises I have made? Where does the strength to keep rising come from? Have you ever fallen? I mean really fallen? Physically? Face down and flat? I cried and fell in my friend's house the other day. Face down and flat. I had a time trying to get up; first of all, to reassure my friend that I was alright and secondly, that I didn't need any help to get up. I was not hurt. I fell on soft carpet. I rolled over, gathered my strength, and got up on all fours.

Yesterday, in talking to one of the male refugees, I noticed he had his feet wrapped in a plastic bag. He had no shoes. I asked him why he had no shoes. He replied he had given them to his son because his son had worn his thin from all the walking. Remembering the Gospel story where Jesus says, "If you have two pair of shoes, one pair belongs to your neighbor." I said to the gentleman, "Here, take my shoes, I think they might fit you." He would not take my shoes for fear I would be left without. I went to my room, lovingly picked up my favorite Birkenstock sandals, and carried them to give to the man. I was hesitant at first. I really didn't want to give my shoes away but in my heart of hearts I was willing to give mine to one who had none. Then God led me to the storeroom where I found a pair of shoes that were an almost perfect fit for the son. The joy in the father's face was radiant when the son returned his shoes. He did not have to take my shoes. There was joy all around!

I was so overwhelmed, that the next day, I went to the shoe store and bought $400 worth of shoes using the money Barbara gave me for the needs of the poor.

The thing is, many people donate clothing: pants, skirts, tops, jackets. Few people donate shoes, underwear, socks, and pajamas. If someone wanted to send a care box, as is the custom in my community, I would ask them to forget the holy cards and candy bars. I would ask for a box of panties and bras, size small. Believe it or not, this would bring such joy to the women and mothers who cross our path each day. Imagine the awesome joy of finally having a clean pair of underwear!

Did I fall a third time, Jesus? Was my heart so hardened that I could not freely give away a second pair of shoes? Will another opportunity be given me to freely give my heart in all I do?

La Navidad está a la vuelta de la esquina. Yo deseo que este día este lleno del amor para, ese niño que va a nacer con un corazón lieno de amor y generoidad.
Christmas is around the corner. I wish for you a day filled with the love of a newborn Child, a heart, loving and generous.

—*Evangeline*

REFLECTION QUESTION

Jesus Falls the Third Time:
How many chances do I get? There is a line in a song, *"I will rise again!"* How am I going to do it?

REFLECTIONS

TENTH STATION
JESUS IS STRIPPED OF HIS GARMENTS

It's Saturday, the 30th of December. Tomorrow will be the last day of 2018. Did we listen to the Word of God each day, or did we just let each day pass us by? Jesus allowed the soldiers to strip Him of His garments. Jesus came into the world naked, but not alone. He had Mary and Joseph, the shepherds, the angels, and the magi following a star, and a dream to welcome His arrival. The refugees come into our country, alone and afraid, following a dream. They arrive cold, hungry, and afraid, and yet with a faith and hope that baffles all of our minds. They arrive and ICE strips them of the little they possess. They are processed and delivered onto the streets. The good people of Annunciation House gather them up in buses, vans, cars, and trucks and bring them to the mercy centers where we feed, house, provide medical assistance, and give them a new set of clothing. We care for their physical well-being. They care for our spiritual, psychological, and emotional well-being.

They give us faith and hope in a God who cares for us all alike. As God brings them out of the violence and abuse in which they lived, God delivers us from the chaos we have made of our lives. As we minister with the refugees, we discover they are psychologically healthy. They know where they have come from. Their pain and suffering have been transforming. They have a plan. They follow a dream. They are focused. We take courage from their focus, their plans, and their dreams. They rise above their suffering and disappointments. They are kind, patient, generous, and loving with each other and with us. The adults are adults, and the children are children.

Yesterday, I gave a child a piece of bread. She thanked me so profoundly and asked God to bless me. My eyes filled up with tears that I had to turn away. I search my heart to remember the time an American child said thank you with such sincerity as hers.

We are who we are, and we try to be all that we are called to be. We have answered the call to feed the hungry, clothe the naked, and free the oppressed. We do it with the great love and generosity of Jesus Christ, our Savior.

Dios bendiga todos sus generosos corazones de amor viviendo con Espíritu para este año que viene.

God bless you all with a generous heart and a loving, living Spirit through the coming year.

—*Evangeline*

REFLECTION QUESTION

Jesus is Stripped of His Garments:
How do I define myself once I have lost everything that defines me?

REFLECTIONS

ELEVENTH STATION
JESUS IS NAILED TO THE CROSS

Slowly the refugees step off the bus with hesitation in their step and fear in their eyes. They don't know who we are or what to expect. We greet them with a handshake and a smile. For a second or two they hesitate, before they return our handshake and liven their faces with a trusting smile. They are the poor, the hungry, and the oppressed, fleeing their country to make for themselves and their children a better life.

Jesus allowed Himself to be nailed to a cold and bitter cross so that these little ones might have a full and fulfilling life. How often have we nailed Jesus to the cross by our indifference and our unwillingness to look at these, His precious wounded children?

In the early days at Nazareth, we fed the refugees. Today, we invite our guests to join us at the table. We break bread together. We eat and join in conversation. We are united in our love for one another and are grateful we are a part of this moment of great suffering and rejoicing in the power of God.

Juan Cortez de la Crux came to us from Honduras. He brought with him his four-year-old son. They have been told that if they bring a child with them, they have a better chance of staying. I don't think it is true, but it is what they believe. Juan left behind a wife, a daughter, and a son. His hope is that someday he will be able to reunite his family in this country. Juan has an engineering degree from the Jesuit University. Someday, Juan will realize his dream if this country will give him a chance.

Let us pray that Juan and so many others will be allowed to follow their dreams. Let us not nail Juan to his cross. I pray and ask you to pray for Juan and his dream to be reunited with his family.

Dios nos bendiga este Año Nuevo con esperanza y tranquilidad.
God bless us in this New Year of hope and tranquility.

—Evangeline

REFLECTION QUESTION

Jesus is Nailed to the Cross:
Whom have I nailed to a cross?

REFLECTIONS

REFLECTIONS

TWELFTH STATION
JESUS DIES ON THE CROSS

Carving and restoring the twelfth station was a challenge. The face of Jesus in His dying stages is impossible to imagine, so I carved the back side of the crucifixion. A coward's choice? Perhaps. Who can look into the face of death and not know death? We have been touched here at Nazareth and in all of El Paso by the death of two very young children. As in the case of Jesus, these deaths were redemptive. How often do we look into the face of the other and not recognize the face of Jesus?

In the beginning, I did not want to take my turn in the medicine room because I was afraid of giving the wrong medicine to a child. I was afraid I would not recognize the signs of dehydration or malnutrition. Some of these children are so tiny to begin with it's hard to know the cause of their sickness.

Juana Maria Cortez, from Honduras, was two months old. Because of a lack of nourishment, her twenty-year-old mother was unable to breastfeed her. They arrived at the center with sixty others, so we did not attend to Maria immediately. Because the baby's crying was almost soundless, she was woefully neglected. Once we realized that both mother and child were very sick, we called a doctor who did pro bono work for us. As soon as she saw how malnourished they were, she called an ambulance to take them to the hospital where she treated them. Four days later, mother and child were on the road to recovery. We made contact with their sponsors to purchase a plane ticket for them to arrive safely at their destination.

We are touched by the daily events of the moment. We don't know who will arrive at our door. All is in the hands of ICE. The number of refugees we receive depends on the number released by ICE. We wait with open arms, a happy smile, and the willingness to do whatever it takes to see the face of Jesus. We show the face of Jesus to those we serve.

Dios bendiga la persona que tu eres hoy. Pon tu frente en alto a Jesús y recuerda que el murió por ti.
God bless you for the person you are today. Look upon the face of Jesus and remember He died for you.

—*Evangeline*

REFLECTION QUESTION

Jesus Dies on the Cross:
It's over.
Who has died because of my neglect or my indifference?

REFLECTIONS

THIRTEENTH STATION
JESUS IS TAKEN DOWN FROM THE CROSS

Never having been a mother, I will never truly know the pain Mary endured as she watched her Son, beaten, mocked, and crucified. I will never know how it feels to hold a dead son in my arms. I can only imagine; yet, I hold Mary and all sorrowing mothers in my heart. How did Jesus feel, knowing the pain He was causing His mother? I feel a hollowed-out pain just to think about these two human beings.

Humanity! What is the cost of being human? Sorrow and tears, an unfulfilling sadness, a helpless, hopeless, tormenting, agonizing feeling that does not go away. Is this what being human means? Pain with a love so great we are willing to endure in order to possess a tiny bit of humanity.

The question everyone asks and wonders about is this: Why would a young father bring a three-year-old daughter with him to seek asylum? We have met them all, young mothers and fathers traveling alone with a young child or children of all ages. Every adult comes with a child. Is the hardship decreased or multiplied by traveling with a son or daughter? The journey has to be difficult traveling alone, but traveling with a child? A parent has to suffer doubly when the child suffers. A parent's task is to try to alleviate the child's pain, and they do. What does a parent do when a four-year-old wears out his/her only pair of shoes? One can only carry a child so far. The weight of a child impedes the progress of the journey.

The answer, of course, is Love. Untiring love, freely given, freely received, a redeeming Love. This is what Mary offered Jesus and Jesus offered His Mother. This is what every refugee delivers to his/her child and what the child gives to the parent. Jesus "in the arms of His Mother" in life as well as death. The refugee "in the arms of the parent" in life and the struggle until death. Oh happy, happy moment!

Ahora debo ir a preparar y servir la cena. Te deseo amor, eterno y redentor.
Now I must go prepare and serve supper. I wish you Love, everlasting and redemptive.

—*Evangeline*

REFLECTION QUESTION

**Jesus is Taken Down from the Cross and
Laid in the Arms of His Blessed Mother:**
The heart has been broken by a love so great that it could not be contained. How do you survive a broken heart or help someone in their hour of greatest need?

REFLECTIONS

FOURTEENTH STATION
JESUS IS LAID IN THE TOMB

It is over, the shouts, the wailing, the tears. All is quiet now. Not even a whisper is heard. The day is spent. How does it feel Jesus to be laid in that cold, dark tomb? You gave everything you had to give and now you can rest in that knowledge. It was a heavy journey and yet there were a lot of good moments. Moments of joy when you heard the children laughing, saw the couples dancing at the wedding feast, and heard the yelp of joy when Peter caught fish.

I believe the tomb teaches us the very difficult lesson of letting go. Tomorrow I will take a break from this ministry of love I have been involved in for the last two and a half months. It has been a great experience of Faith and Hope, Courage and Perseverance, Sorrow and Joy, and always a journey of Not Enough. I didn't have enough arms to hug all the beautiful people who touched my life. I didn't have enough time to finish the work that had to be done. I didn't know enough about cooking to help with the meals. I didn't have enough stamina to go beyond the time allotted. I wonder today if I had been twenty years younger, would I have been able to do more? There is a great difference, after all, between starting at thirty and starting again at almost eighty.

I have to let go of thinking I might have done more if this or that had been the case. This is who I am, and this is what I gave; love, patience, tears and prayer, all I had. I couldn't have done it alone. I have to let go of what I might have given or what might have been. I did my best and now I must lay it to rest.

Jesus has been laid in the tomb. It is enough.

Les deseo un corazón abierto, lágrimas y un amor tan grande que cambiará el mundo.
I wish for you an open heart, tears, and a love so great it will change the world.
—*Evangeline*

REFLECTION QUESTION

Jesus is Laid in the Tomb:
Was it enough? Did I do enough? What more can I do?

REFLECTIONS

REFLECTIONS

FIFTEENTH STATION
THE RESURRECTION OF JESUS - PART 1

Dear God, it's so hot and the people come to us burnt, tired, and hungry. We had 46 today. A small number, if you compare it with the 300 we were getting daily in November, December, and January.

Because we are getting fewer numbers of people, we have fewer volunteers and so the work piles up. In the past, we were asked to do intake, make telephone calls to connect the families with their sponsors, and one or two other things. Today we are asked to do these tasks, plus wash sheets and towels, hang them outside to dry, and later fold and put away. We are also asked to prepare a meal, serve it, and clean up. As a staff coordinator, I must attend to all the jobs and make sure all the jobs are taken care of in a timely manner.

The people coming to us are beautiful. They all come with stories full of pain and sorrow. Many are so young and have suffered so much at the hands of people they trusted. I listen to the tears in their voices and wish I were a miracle healer. How did Jesus do it? Listening to the voices full of sorrow, looking at the scarred faces of His friends and neighbors. And I must ask myself, where is the love that should bring us together? Where is the hope and faith that all will be well?

My friend Blanca Arellano came to El Paso yesterday, and together with her daughter, Susie, we traveled to Juarez to look at the situation from the other side of the border. Oh, my sweet Jesus, how your heart must break as you look at the worse than awful conditions these people must endure. Over 500 persons crowded in a very small space, no chairs; all must sit on the floor. Very little food, limited amounts of drinking water, no showers, no place to wash their face or brush their teeth. The babies can't stop crying, the young children clutch their parents' bodies, and the teenagers just stand around with gloomy faces. The people are afraid to stay, and they are afraid to go out of the site and return to their homes. The predators are waiting to grab them and use them for their own gains and purposes. What a terrible place to be!

I was planning to think and write the last Station of the Cross; The Resurrection; however, I find myself to be without words. There is no Resurrection here today. Maybe . . . tomorrow.

Les mando amor	*I send you love*
Pido sus oraciones	*Ask for prayers*
Fe y esperanza	*Faith and hope*
Para todo la gente	*For the people*

—*Evangeline Salazar, OSB*

REFLECTIONS

FIFTEENTH STATION
THE RESURRECTION OF JESUS - PART 2

It would be lovely if we could declare resurrection now for the refugees, migrants, and asylum seekers; however, it seems, the time is not yet.

Jesus rose from the dead after much suffering at the hands of those who were afraid of Him and those who betrayed Him. He was persecuted by the mobs, the unknowing, the prejudiced, and those in power who were afraid that Jesus would diminish their power. How sad! Suffer He did. He was tortured and died on a cross made by human hands. And He rose from the dead. Resurrection!

Today, in this very place of shelter, next to a detention center, we can hear the cry of the poor. Yesterday, they brought into the center a man in a wheelchair. He tried to escape from the detention center by jumping over a barbed wire fence. He fell and broke a hip and a leg.

In our shelter, is a woman, Soledad, who is three months pregnant and free to travel to Chicago where she has a sponsor and a court date. However, her husband is held in the detention center with no exit in sight. Soledad has a dilemma: Should she go and leave her husband behind? Or should she stay at the shelter, forfeit her date in court, and a possible freedom pass to stay in the United States?

I am so saddened by the inhumane treatment of those who seek legal migration and asylum. The many who are detained in ICE detention facilities are separated from their friends and families, forced into cages with no knowledge of how long they will be detained. They have not committed any crimes, yet they are incarcerated for whatever time their jailers deem adequate- weeks, months, or even years.

The resurrection of Jesus happened after much suffering. I pray and I ask us all to call upon God to lift the chains that bind the refugees and asylum seekers.

Thank you to the people and groups who are working to help the asylum seekers: Sara Jackson in Aurora, Colorado; RAICES; Stephen Michael Tumolo; ACLU; and so many more.

Resurrection!

REFLECTIONS